Denise Justice-France

F.E.A.R.

by

Denise Justice-France

ISBN-13: 978-1511776394

ISBN-10: 1511776390

F.E.A.R.

When you see the word F.E.A.R. Look at it as an opportunity to do more, to be more, to become more. REVERSE THAT WORD AND REPLACE IT WITH.

F. FREEDOM

E. EMPOWER

A. AWARE

R. REWARD

You will receive Freedom from all your fears, freedom from all your worries, freedom from the depression and anxiety. You will receive Freedom. Yes I said Freedom. Because the opposite of Fear is FREEDOM.

Your FEARS WILL turn into excellent opportunities that are open to you, doors will open just like you command it to open. You will have the freedom to do whatever you wanted to do. Why?

Because you let go of the fear from doing it.

You will become Empower to do more to become more
and you will have the strength and the ability to say, BOY
I did it. It was not so hard. That fear was only a blocking
thing that was trying to block me from moving forward.
See God will tell you it is time to Let go, it is time to
move forward. The only thing that is stopping you is
FEAR.

This is Satan way to stop you!

The thief comes only to kill, to steal and destroy. But,
God come that you may have life and have it more
abundantly. John 10:10

God empower you to move on, He empower you to go

forward. God did not say stay the same.

Now unto to him who is able to do exceedingly above all

that I can ask or think according to the power that

worketh in us. Ephesians 3:20

God lives in you and me; he is the force behind

everything we can do. If you trust in him, Nothing is

impossible. Luke 1:37

You are Empower.

You become AWARE of you who are and you are aware

of the power that you have inside of you, which is God.

You are aware of your limitations and your weakness because everyone has weakness. That when Satan tries to attack you at your weakness times. But when you should become aware of the power of God inside of you and you must TURN IN AROUND AND YOU MUST READ THE SCRIPTURES AND BECOME AWARE OF GOD INSIDE OF YOU.

You will tell the Fear, You will tell the problem, you will tell the situation to FLEE.

Because In the Name of Jesus. And it will flee. You are Free from the problem, yOu are Empower and you Aware of the Results and the Reward that you will Received.

That's the Reward. You are Free. You have FREEDOM.

So the next time F.E.A.R. come knocking on your door

remember to turn it around.

To Freedom,

To Empower

To Aware

To Reward to your new Results.

2 Timothy 1:7 (ASV) For God gave us not a spirit of

fearfulness; but of power and love and discipline

Matthew 19:26

Jesus looked at them and said, "With man this is

impossible, but with God all things are possible."

The next time FEAR come write down what you are afraid of?

Then write down the solution.

The next time FEAR come write down what you are

afraid of.

Then write down the solution

The next time FEAR come write down what you are afraid of?

Then write down the solution

The next time FEAR come write down what you are

afraid of?

Then write down the solution

The next time FEAR come write down what you are

afraid Of?.

Then write down the solution

The next time FEAR come write down what you are

afraid Of?.

Then write down the solution

The next time FEAR come write down what you are

afraid Of?.

Then write down the solution

Fear is Over. Opportunities are OPEN>

The New the Impossible.

Fear is Over. Opportunities are OPEN>

The New the Impossible

Fear is Over. Opportunities are OPEN>

The New the Impossible

Fear is Over. Opportunities are OPEN>

The New the Impossible

FREEDOM

EMPOWER

AWARE

REWARD

MY NEW RESULTS.